Making + MATH + *Work*

How Much Is Infinity?

BY JOY VISTO

CREATIVE EDUCATION

CREATIVE PAPERBACKS

Published by Creative Education and Creative Paperbacks
P.O. Box 227, Mankato, Minnesota 56002
Creative Education and Creative Paperbacks
are imprints of The Creative Company
www.thecreativecompany.us

Design and production by Liddy Walseth
Art direction by Rita Marshall
Printed in the United States of America

Photographs by Corbis (176/Ocean, JGI/Jamie Grill/Blend Images, Lindsay Kelley/Tetra Images,
Ken Welsh/Design Pics), Dreamstime (Anphotos, Azurita, Dreamer82, Daniel Oravec,
Rangizzz), iStockphoto (bbeltman, Jill Chen, collinkyla, Ericlefrancais, gyener, herreid,
Alexey Ivanov, luiscarlosjimenez, MileA, OSTILL, PhotographerOlympus, Synergee,
taoty, tiridifilm, ZargonDesign), Shutterstock (creatOR76, Olga Danylenko, Claudio Divizia,
Gyvafoto, harper kt, Kamenuka, Arkady Mazor, ostill, Tribalium)

Library of Congress Cataloging-in-Publication Data
Visto, Joy.
How much is infinity? / Joy Visto.
p. cm. – (Making math work)
Includes bibliographical references and index.
Summary: A helpful guide for understanding the mathematical concepts and real-world
applications of arithmetic, including classroom tips, common terms such as quotients, and
exercises to encourage hands-on practice.
ISBN 978-1-60818-572-6 (hardcover)
ISBN 978-1-62832-173-9 (pbk)
1. Arithmetic—Juvenile literature. 2. Cardinal numbers—Juvenile literature. I. Title.

QA115.V57 2015
513.2—dc23   2014034725

CCSS: RI.5.1, 2, 3, 8; RI.6.1, 2, 3, 4, 5, 6, 7; RST.6-8.3, 4, 6, 7

First Edition HC 9 8 7 6 5 4 3 2 1
First Edition PBK 9 8 7 6 5 4 3 2 1

When you think about mathematics, you probably think about a class at school where you do **calculations** and answer word problems. But have you ever thought about math being all around you? It's in every shape and pattern you see. It's in every song you hear. It's in every game you play and any puzzle you solve! The first mathematicians realized this, and they looked for ways to prove it—to show how order and reason could explain much about life as they knew it. Sometimes this was easy to do. But other times, people just didn't get it. Even some of the most intelligent people in history have struggled with math: Albert Einstein once wrote to a child, "Do not worry about your difficulties in Mathematics. I can assure you mine are still greater."

So how can you use whatever you know about math in everyday life? When you *count* the number of minutes your teacher takes to tell you about a homework assignment, *add* up the friends you've invited to your house after school, or *divide* the tasks in a group project, you are using math! In such cases, you are using a type of math known as arithmetic. This is the oldest branch of mathematics, and it is all about numbers and quantities. *How much* math can you make work using arithmetic?

Prominent American Series

ALBERT EINSTEIN 8c

MATHEMATICIAN–PHYSICIST
NOBEL PRIZE WINNER
1879–1955

Artmaster

First Day of Issue

THE ANCIENT EGYPTIANS
MADE THEIR HOME
ALONG THE NILE RIVER
(OPPOSITE).

BASICS OF BASE-10

WHEN DID YOU START using math? It was probably when you learned to count. You started by counting to 10, and then to 100. Next, you learned how to write numbers. That is the same process people have used for thousands of years. They began by counting everyday objects and then wrote numbers to share their counts with others. One of the most basic systems for writing numbers was the tally system. In this system, a tally mark represents the number one. It is easy to understand at first but can quickly become difficult to follow, as larger numbers require many tallies. Therefore, it eventually became necessary to find ways to shorten numeric representations.

One of the earliest civilizations to have a written language, the Egyptians, wrote their numbers just like they wrote everything else—with pictures called hieroglyphs. Some of the pictures make sense to us, like using a tally for the number one. Others seem a little strange, such as the "astonished man" that represents 1,000,000. In hieroglyphs, the number "1,126" would be written like this:

As new civilizations rose to power in the regions around Egypt, they developed different writing systems and, eventually, alphabets. Different societies developed their own number systems, which involved unique symbols and counting methods. Between 2000 and 200 B.C., in the area known as Mesopotamia (present-day Iraq), the Babylonian system originated.

The Babylonians used a place value system in which symbols' values were determined by their order, or place. Instead of **base-10**, the Babylonians used a sexigesimal system, which is similar to what we use to divide 1 minute into 60 seconds. They used symbols called wedges to represent 1

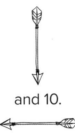

and 10.

All the numbers were written using a combination of those two wedges. Then they were grouped to show their position in base-60. To write "1,126," you would do this:

The development of number systems was not limited to western Europe and Asia. Across the ocean, the Maya used a place value system based on the number 20. The Maya used a _____ for the number 5 and ● to represent 1. They were the first to use a symbol for zero. Mathematicians in other parts of the world struggled with how to represent zero. They did not understand why they would need a symbol for "nothing." However, the Maya saw its usefulness when a certain place had no quantity represented in it. The most common Maya representation for zero was a shell. Because the Maya were so far away, their number system did not impact the mathematicians of Europe, though.

Instead, ancient Romans had the greatest influence on Western math. The Romans began using what we recognize as letters for their numbers in the 7th century B.C. There are two main theories about the origin of Roman numerals. The first relates to the previously mentioned tally system. In the Roman tally system, every 5th tally was double-marked (V or Λ) and every 10th tally was crosscut (X). It is argued that the basic Roman numerals for 1, 5, and 10 come from this process. The second theory involves hand signals, such as holding up one finger to mean 1. Although neither explanation refers to letters exactly, it is easiest to discuss Roman numerals by referencing the individual letters used.

Unlike the Babylonian and Maya place value systems, the Romans used an additive system. A number's value came from adding the values represented by each letter. There is also a subtraction component to this system. To avoid writing one number more than four times, the smaller number is placed in front of the bigger number to show subtraction. The number nine, for instance, was written as IX to signify 10 minus 1. And 99 had to be written as XCIX (XC for 90 and IX for 9). Roman numerals may have looked more like a spelling test, but the Romans were able to write every number except zero.

All those systems eventually gave way to the one we use today, the Hindu-Arabic system. This was developed by people in India sometime before A.D. 600. They introduced it to Arabs in the Middle East who adopted it and applied it to **algebra**. Arab scholar Muhammad ibn Musa al-Khwarizmi was especially influential in the spread of Hindu-Arabic numerals, as his works were translated into Latin—the language common to European regions of the time.

Just like the Egyptians and Romans, the Hindu-Arabic numerals that you know use what is called base-10. Why would so many numerical systems be based on 10 numbers? It's simple, really—people all over the world can count to 10 using the fingers on their hands. (Even the base for the Maya number system, 20, represents the number of fingers and toes.) In fact, the word *digit* comes from the Latin word for "finger." If we didn't have thumbs, we might be living in a base-8 world. Now that would be different!

As the Hindu-Arabic system became the standard for writing numbers, mathematicians began looking for ways to simplify the process of calculations done with them. One of the earliest tools was the abacus. This was a board with beads or other parts that could be moved. The position of a particular bead would designate if it was in the ones, tens, or another place. Later on, Scottish mathematician John Napier developed a calculating machine out of rods made from ivory. These rods could be turned to calculate answers for multiplication and division. Nicknamed "Napier's Bones," this device gave way to the slide rule and, eventually, the computer.

Thanks to rapid advancements in technology since the 1800s, mathematicians have been able to search for new numbers. Some numbers can be divided by only themselves and one. These are called prime numbers. (Numbers that can be divided by additional numbers are composite.) Ancient Greek mathematicians believed prime numbers had a mystical significance. In 300 B.C., Euclid proved that there is an **infinite** number of primes. Yet mathematicians continue to look for prime numbers. Now they use computers to help in the search. The largest prime numbers are more than 17 million digits long!

10
20
30
40

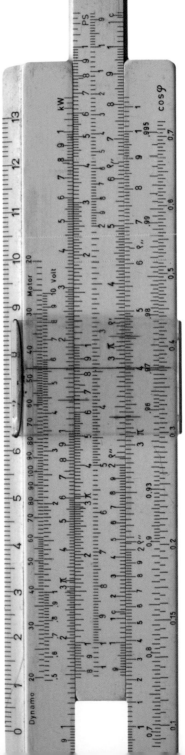

In addition to being prime or composite, numbers can be classified according to different characteristics they share, such as whether they are even or odd. Even numbers can be divided in half. If you have an even number of cookies, then you and a friend would each get the same amount—assuming you share! An odd number means that there will be some left over.

A third way we put numbers into groups is by sets. The most basic set of numbers is the counting, or natural, numbers. The numbers 1, 2, 3, 4, etc. are for counting objects, but they do not work in every situation. For instance, 0 is a number, but it's not a natural number. It is part of a different set—the whole numbers. If you add in the opposites of the natural numbers, the negative numbers, you get the set of integers. None of the numbers in these sets has a **fraction** or **decimal** attached to them.

Fractions are important for representing parts of a quantity, like when you have to split a birthday cake among friends. Fractions and decimals, when written with the integers, form the set of rational numbers. Every rational number can be written as a fraction. Numbers such as ½ or ¾ or .56 fit into the rational numbers. Other numbers, such as pi, cannot be written as fractions because their decimals go on forever.

When you combine the rational and the irrational numbers, you finally end up with all the **real numbers**. In school, you spend most of your time with the whole numbers, the rational numbers, and the integers. Did you know there are as many whole numbers as there are rational numbers or integers? There is an infinite amount in each set! If you started counting today, you could count for the rest of your life and never be done. From the origins of the astonished man in Egyptian numerals to our familiar Hindu-Arabic system, numbers have changed drastically. However, the calculations we can do with them remain the same.

Base-2

While base-10 may be the base for numbers, computers have adopted base-2 for their operations. In binary, the two digits are 0 and 1. They represent a switch turning on (1) and off (0). Computations can be done with numbers written in this way, and in fact, that is why the machines are called computers. Considering how much computers rely on it, base-2 may soon become more popular in today's world than base-10.

PEMDAS: THE ORDER OF ARITHMETIC

THE ABILITY TO COUNT makes it possible to do so many things. However, being able to calculate is an even more valuable skill. There are many different operations that you can do with numbers, from addition and subtraction to multiplication and division. Just as repeated addition gives multiplication and repeated subtraction gives division, these simple operations can be used to make more complex ones. Exponents and factorials are forms of repeated multiplication, while square roots and other radicals are repeated division.

The first operation you probably learned was addition. You practiced finding the sum, or the answer to an addition problem. When you were younger, adding probably meant counting with your fingers or taking your socks off so that you could use your toes, too! After doing many problems, you probably had most of your addition facts memorized. You could do problems in your head, adding 2 plus 7 or 21 plus 13.

Learning to subtract was the next step in learning to calculate. Maybe your teacher told you that addition and subtraction are opposites, a lot like hot and cold or tall and short. Addition and subtraction can undo, or cancel out, one another. If you add a number and then subtract that same number, the **difference** will be the original number. For instance, adding five to four, then subtracting five from that sum, gives an answer of four.

TWO *PLUS* SEVEN

What happens when you add 2 numbers that give a total greater than 10? Because you do math in a base-10 system, you will need to carry a 1 into the tens column. A similar process happens in subtraction—but because subtraction is the opposite of addition, the process of carrying is replaced by borrowing. In a subtraction problem like 21 minus 13, it is difficult to subtract 3 from 1 in the ones column. Instead, you must borrow a 10 from the 20. The borrowed 10 makes the problem in the ones column 11 minus 3, which then makes it much easier to find the difference (8).

Another pair of opposite operations is multiplication and division. Multiplication can be thought of as repeated addition. If you had to explain to someone how to multiply 6 by 3, you might tell him to add three sixes together. Because multiplication is rooted in addition, there are patterns that you can identify and memorize. The more you work with multiplication, the easier it becomes to know your facts rather than rely on adding numbers together over and over again. If you're in a pinch, though, just think of adding. It might be tough to do 46 times 2 in your head, but do you think you could add 46 and 46? Whenever you can simplify a problem that initially looks too challenging, you'll be less likely to get stuck.

Sometimes the tougher problems can really give people trouble, though. Of all the operations, division is probably the most difficult. But think of it this way: division is repeated subtraction. If your friend wanted to know how to divide 6 by 3, you might tell her to subtract 3 from 6 until she got to 0. Six divided by 3 could be written this way: 6 minus 3 minus 3 equals 0. Because you were able to subtract 3 from 6 twice, 6 divided by 3 is 2.

Using repeated subtraction is also helpful in calculating the remainder, the amount left over after dividing. The remainder is an important part of a division problem because not every number can be nicely divided. For example, every odd number gives a remainder of 1 when you divide it by 2. If you subtract 2 from an odd number as many times as you can, you will always have 1 left at the end. One is the remainder. Take a look at the following example: 5 minus 2 minus 2 equals 1.

However, the best way to *start* a division problem is to know whether you will end up with a remainder. To help you recognize if a number can be divided by certain **divisors**, see the hints at right. They are listed for the numbers 1 to 10. How many of these did you know? How many were new?

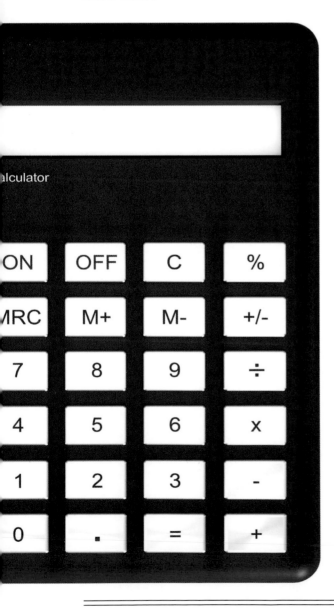

alculator

ON	OFF	C	%
MRC	M+	M-	+/-
7	8	9	÷
4	5	6	x
1	2	3	-
0	.	=	+

1: Every number is divisible by one! The answer will always be the original number.

2: To be divisible by 2, the number must be even! Even numbers end in 2, 4, 6, 8, or 0.

3: If the sum of the digits of a number is divisible by 3, the original number is divisible by 3.

4: To be divisible by 4, the last two digits of the number must be divisible by 4.

5: Numbers that end in 5 or 0 are divisible by 5.

6: Numbers that are even and have digits that add up to a sum that is divisible by 3 are divisible by 6.

7: Remove the last digit from the number, then subtract its double from that new number. If that number is divisible by 7, then the original number is divisible by 7.

8: To be divisible by 8, the last 3 digits of a number must be divisible by 8.

9: If the sum of the digits of a number is divisible by 9, the original number is divisible by 9.

10: Any number whose last digit is 0 is divisible by 10.

Look at the numbers below, and apply the divisibility rules to them. (They may have divisors other than the numbers 1 to 10. But for now, just check for divisibility using those numbers.)

136   **2,160**   **495**   **5,061** *

Did you notice that zero was not listed in the divisibility rules? If you enter any number into a calculator and attempt to divide it by zero, you can get some strange results. Most calculators will give an error symbol, but others will give the infinity symbol, ∞. How could dividing by zero give an answer as big as infinity?

It has to do with patterns that happen when you divide. If you divide by a number greater than 1, the **quotient** is always a smaller number. If you divide by 1, you get the same number back. What happens if you divide by a number smaller than 1, like ½, ¼, or ⅛? As you divide by smaller and smaller numbers, the answer gets bigger and bigger! When you approach dividing by

*Answer Key: Problem A

CHECKING FOR LOWEST TERMS

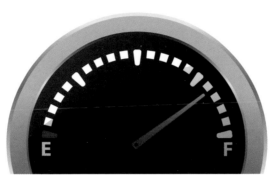

IF YOU HAVE A CALCULATOR HANDY, punch in 29 divided by 4. Did you get 7.25? When you divide 29 in your head, you probably calculate 7 with a remainder of 1. Your calculator is giving the same answer, but calculators have a different way of handling remainders. When you are getting a remainder of one, that one still needs to be divided by four. Your calculator does that division and gets .25, which is the decimal representation of the fraction ¼.

Fractions are made up of a numerator, which is the number on top, over a denominator, the number on the bottom. The numerator is the number being divided, while the denominator is what it is being divided by. Fractions appear in a variety of places. In math, they show up as you calculate **probability** or measure **slope**. In your life, you may have used fractions in recipes or in figuring out how much gas is left in a tank. Every division problem can be written as a fraction. So that's why 1 divided by 4 can look like ¼.

A TYPICAL FUEL GAUGE SHOWS THE DRIVER WHAT FRACTION OF GAS IS LEFT.

$$\frac{3}{4} \div \frac{5}{8} \qquad \frac{2}{5} \div \frac{10}{19} \qquad \frac{4}{7} \div \frac{3}{8} \; *$$

Now for the tricky part. In order to add or subtract with fractions, you need to start by making the denominators match. What you are looking for is the smallest number that is a multiple of both denominators. This is called the least common multiple. If you cannot find the smallest one, you can still do the calculation. Just know that you will have to do some reducing at the end.

Fractions are pieces of a whole. If the denominators are not the same, the pieces are different sizes. You need to make the pieces the same size so that you can put them together.

To help identify the least common multiple for two denominators, make a list of all the multiples for both denominators, stopping when they share one. In the example below, you can see how this is done.

Find common denominators for ⅚ and ¾.
Multiples of six: 6, 12, 18, 24, ...
Multiples of four: 4, 8, 12, 16, 20, ...
The two numbers share a common multiple of 12.

The fractions must be modified so that they both have the new denominator. To do this without changing the value of the fraction, you must multiply both numerator and denominator by the same number. That number is determined by dividing the least common multiple by the original denominator. The quotient is what you will multiply with in order to change the fraction. Continuing with the example from before, you can see how that is done on page 32.

*Answer Key: Problem E

Change $\frac{5}{6}$ by multiplying the numerator and denominator by **2**, the quotient of **12** divided by **6**.

$$(5 \times 2)/(6 \times 2) = {}^{10}\!/_{12}$$

Change $\frac{3}{4}$ by multiplying the numerator and denominator by **3**, the quotient of **12** divided by **4**.

$$(3 \times 3)/(4 \times 3) = {}^{9}\!/_{12}$$

Now that you have common denominators for both fractions, you can add or subtract the numerators. The denominator stays the same throughout. Returning to the previous examples, here is what it would look like to add $\frac{5}{6}$ and $\frac{3}{4}$ or subtract those fractions:

$\frac{5}{6} + \frac{3}{4}$ $\frac{5}{6} - \frac{3}{4}$

${}^{10}\!/_{12} + {}^{9}\!/_{12}$ ${}^{10}\!/_{12} - {}^{9}\!/_{12}$

${}^{19}\!/_{12}$ ${}^{1}\!/_{12}$

In the problems below, make sure you have common denominators before going any farther. You cannot do any adding or subtracting until you have common denominators. At the end, check to see if your answer is in lowest terms.

$\frac{3}{8} + \frac{1}{2}$ $\frac{5}{6} - \frac{1}{4}$ ${}^{11}\!/_{18} - \frac{1}{3}$ $\frac{1}{3} + \frac{1}{5}$ *

Answer Key: Problem F

There are different types of fractions. The most common kind is called a proper fraction. In a proper fraction, the number in the numerator is less than the number in the denominator. There are also improper fractions. In an improper fraction, the numerator is greater than the denominator. Improper fractions can be reduced to mixed numbers. A mixed number has a whole number part and a fraction part. For example, in 7 1/4, seven is the whole number, and 1/4 is the fraction. The fraction part of a mixed number will always be proper.

Most of what you are taught about fractions is explained using proper fractions. What is nice about fractions is that the patterns and skills that you learn for proper fractions carry over into improper fractions and mixed numbers. If you can master the skills with proper fractions, you will have no trouble with fractions of any type.

It is important to be able to do all the different operations with fractions, especially for cases when working with decimals is not feasible. A great example of this is when you are cooking. Measuring cups give amounts in fractions based on one cup. If you want to double a recipe or cut it in half, you will need to know how to work with those fractions. If you are trying to determine how much pizza you need to order for you and some friends, you will need to be able to add what fraction of a whole pizza each person can eat. Once you master the rules for each operation, you will be able to tackle any fraction problem!

Measuring cups GIVE AMOUNTS IN FRACTIONS *based on one cup.*

NUMBERS OUT OF ABSURDITY

ONE OF THE LAST SETS OF NUMBERS TO BE ACCEPTED as valid by mathematicians was the integers. The integers represent all the whole numbers and their opposites (the negative numbers).

LEIBNIZ IS ALSO CREDITED FOR HIS WORK ON THE MODERN BINARY SYSTEM.

Fractions do not belong in the set of integers.

Until the 17th century, numbers were thought of primarily in terms of length. For example, the number 2 was often pictured as a segment that was two units long. Mathematicians could not picture a length of -2, and as a result, they did not include these numbers in their calculations. Usually the only time a negative number was used was when it stood for a loss, as when someone lost money. It was not until Gottfried Leibniz began his work in **calculus** in the late 1600s that mathematicians really accepted negative numbers and stopped referring to them as "absurd."

You may agree with that attitude of some of history's greatest mathematicians such as Blaise Pascal and Girolamo Cardano, two of the devel-

opers of probability and statistics. However, in today's world, negative numbers show up all over the place. You may have already had a lot of experience with what they are. For example, on a cold morning in winter when the temperature is below zero, it is a negative value. If you have played golf, you know that a score below par is measured with a negative number.

A negative number is the opposite of a positive number. It can also be defined as the "additive inverse" of a positive number. This means that when a negative number is added to the same positive, the sum will always be zero. They cancel each other out.

Because adding with negative numbers can be somewhat challenging, try thinking of them in terms of opposites. Just as positive and negative numbers are opposites, so are addition and subtraction. In fact, subtraction is often defined as "adding the opposite." Therefore, adding the opposite number is similar to subtraction. Read through the following examples to see how this idea can be applied to numbers.

-2 + -3   **This problem can be thought of as subtracting 2 and subtracting 3 for a total of subtracting 5, or a sum of -5.**

-7 + 12   **This problem can be thought of as subtracting 7 and adding 12. Together, these operations equal adding 5, which gives a total of 5.**

To understand negative numbers, it can be helpful to visualize them by using their position on a number line. Negative numbers are plotted to the left of zero. Numbers that are farther left are less than the numbers that are to the right. Take the numbers 3 and 5, for example. On a number line, 3 is to the left of 5. Now think of -3 and -5. You might want to say that -3 < -5, but -5 is to the left of -3, and therefore the correct inequality would be -5 < -3. Picturing that number line can help you in performing integer operations.

Another way people think of positive and negative numbers is in terms of steps. If you are dealing with a negative number, that represents taking steps

Four 4s

An interesting series of calculations can happen with four 4s. Using any operations you want—but only four 4s—you can compute all the whole numbers up to 100. For example, 4 + 4 - 4 + 4 = 12. You can also use four factorial (4!), which is equal to 24: 4! + 4! + 4! + 4! = 96. How many numbers can you make while following these rules?

SUBTRACTION *IS OFTEN* DEFINED AS *ADDING THE* OPPOSITE

The two students got different answers in the problems below. See if you can spot the error that was made by one of the students.

Student A
-6 ÷ -2 + -3 × 5 - -2
3 + -15 - -2
3 + 15 + 2
20

Student B
-6 ÷ -2 + -3 × 5 - -2
3 + -15 - -2
3 + -15 + 2
-10

Anytime you do a problem involving negative numbers, you need to be mindful of the signs. Unfortunately, wrong answers can come from mis-reading or miswriting a sign. And when some part gets messed up, it can affect the entire outcome! In the example above, Student A did great work with the calculations in line two, but from that line to the next, a negative symbol was lost. Instead of arriving at the correct answer (-10), Student A was off by 30!

Remember to work carefully with symbols and numbers. It's important to understand how a number can fit within a specific set of numbers, such as the negative numbers or fractions. Much of arithmetic is in understanding numbers. If you can recognize how numbers fit into sets, it will help you do arithmetic. How can you get better at recognizing these things? Practice! Try thinking up different numbers in your head and see where they fit. As you do more and more calculations, you will become a more confident mathematician!

Remember to WORK CAREFULLY WITH SYMBOLS *and numbers.*

MATH TOOLKIT

1. Although the abacus, slide rule, and Napier's Bones helped mathematicians calculate with greater speed and accuracy, the computer has been the most influential technological development. Today, it's hard to imagine life without computers. However, just as recently as the 1950s, computers looked very different. They were often the size of large rooms and weighed nearly 30 tons (27.2 t). As computers have slimmed down, they have become more powerful. They are valuable tools for mathematicians and for you!

2. The factorial (!) calculation multiplies all the counting numbers up to a given limit. If you want to arrange five books on a shelf, you have five choices for which book should come first. Then four books with four options, then three, then two, then one in the final spot. In this case, $5! = 5 \times 4 \times 3 \times 2 \times 1$, where you have 120 different ways to arrange your books.

3. If you ever get stuck when finding a common denominator for two fractions, don't worry; there's a trick! When in doubt, you can always multiply the two denominators. Continue the rest of the problem the same way as before. The catch is that your denominator may not be in lowest terms. If not, you will need to reduce your fraction at the end. Simplifying the fraction is especially important when you choose this strategy.

4. When you look at a calculator, there are two buttons that look like negative symbols. However, one of those buttons is the subtraction key. When you try to use this as a negative button, your calculator will kick out an error message. Also, some calculators want you to put the number in first, and then push the negative symbol. Practice with your calculator to find out how it likes to operate!

GLOSSARY

algebra: a branch of mathematics that uses letters and numbers to solve for unknown values in different equations

base-10: a number system that uses ten symbols (0, 1, 2, 3, 4, 5, 6, 7, 8, 9) to create any number; in this system, each place represents a specific power of ten

binary: relating to a number that is written in a base-2 setting using only 0 and 1

calculations: operations performed on numbers

calculus: a branch of mathematics that studies change, usually on an infinitely small level

decimal: numbers after a decimal point; a form of fraction where the denominator is a power of ten

difference: the answer to a subtraction problem

divisors: numbers by which a particular number will be divided

factor: a number that is multiplied in a multiplication problem; also, a number that evenly divides a given number

fraction: a number that relates pieces of a whole quantity by division

infinite: without end, such as numbers that can be counted forever

lowest terms: describing fractions whose numerators and denominators do not have any factors in common

probability: a branch of mathematics that involves determining the likelihood of a particular event

products: answers for multiplication problems

quotient: the answer for a division problem

real numbers: the set of numbers that includes the whole numbers, integers, rational numbers, and irrational numbers; each real number can be represented on a number line

slope: the measure of how steep a line is, calculated by the fraction rise/run

squaring: the process of multiplying a number by itself; represented with an exponent of two

SELECTED BIBLIOGRAPHY

Berlinghoff, William P., and Fernando Q. Gouvêa. *Math through the Ages: A Gentle History for Teachers and Others.* Washington, D.C.: MAA Service Center, 2004.

Fuson, Karen Connors. "Decimal system." *World Book Advanced.*

Kaplan, Robert. *The Nothing That Is: A Natural History of Zero.* Oxford: Oxford University Press, 2000.

Liebeck, Martin. *A Concise Introduction to Pure Mathematics.* Boca Raton: Taylor & Francis, 2006.

Rooney, Anne. *The Story of Mathematics.* London: Arcturus, 2008.

Struik, Dirk J. *A Concise History of Mathematics.* New York: Dover, 1987.

WEBSITES

Cyberchase: Find It Fractions

http://pbskids.org/cyberchase/find-it/fractions/

Watch videos to learn more about numerators, denominators, and other fun fraction facts.

Roman Numerals

http://www.roman-numerals.org/index.html

Use games, quizzes, and other materials to practice writing with Roman numerals.

Problem F

$\frac{3}{8} + \frac{1}{2}$

$\frac{3}{8} + (1 \times 4)/(2 \times 4)$

$\frac{3}{8} + \frac{4}{8}$

$\frac{7}{8}$

$\frac{5}{6} - \frac{1}{4}$

$(5 \times 2)/(6 \times 2) - (1 \times 3)/(4 \times 3)$

$\frac{10}{12} - \frac{3}{12}$

$\frac{7}{12}$

$\frac{11}{18} - \frac{1}{3}$

$\frac{11}{18} - (1 \times 6)/(3 \times 6)$

$\frac{11}{18} - \frac{6}{18}$

$\frac{5}{18}$

$\frac{1}{3} + \frac{1}{5}$

$(1 \times 5)/(3 \times 5) - (1 \times 3)/(5 \times 3)$

$\frac{5}{15} - \frac{3}{15}$

$\frac{2}{15}$

Problem G

-3 + -5

-8

-7 + 3

-4

10 + -4

6

Problem H

5 - -6

5 + 6

11

8 - 10

8 + -10

-2

-2 - 6

-2 + -6

-8

Problem I

8 × -3 = -24

-5 × -4 = 20

-35 ÷ -5 = 7

-54 ÷ 6 = -9